Goal Your way To a Successful Happy Marriage

Ready Set Goal

By: Rebecca DuBose

Copyright © 2021 Rebecca DuBose

All rights reserved

No part of this book may be reproduced, or stored in a retrieval system, or transmitted in any form or by any means, electronic, mechanical, photocopying, recording, or otherwise, without express written permission of the publisher.

ISBN-13: 978-0-578-84830-3

Cover Photo Taken By: Beige Brother Photography

Library of Congress Control Number: 2021903042

Printed in the United States of America

Disclaimer

The author, Rebecca DuBose or the Publisher, Wisdom Writes LLC holds no liability in the outcome of your relationship, marriage, self-care, or decisions. Make your own decisions and do what is best for you, your family, and your relationships.

Dedication

This is to my loving husband and king in our sacred union,

Kelinski DuBose Sr.

Thank you for teaching me, showing me new things, and taking care of me. Taking care of the innermost things that I left unknowingly unattended. For being my ace boon coon. My business partner and investor. My homie lover and best friend. I appreciate you for every prayer that has gone up on my behalf as I continue to grow daily. Your patience, endurance, faith, and belief in me have released me from many years of bondage. Thank you for taking your heart and wrapping it around my soul. Keeping me grounded in my walk with you as we go on our God-appointed journey together. I thank God for you every day. You are a light that stays lit so even when I feel like I can't find my way you continue to feed my soul and tell me just how valuable I am and how much you want me or need me. Thank you with all my love.

Proverbs 18:22 (AMP)

He who finds a [true and faithful] wife finds a good thing and obtains favor and approval from the Lord.

Dedication

To my loving 7 children:

Thank you for teaching me, love. For teaching me that holding you in my arms would change my world. It would change my understanding of lean not unto my own understanding. It has shown me how strong I am even in the midst of being challenged on multiple levels. Your presence has given me the opportunity to never be selfish. With your innocence and outspoken voices, I've learned that even when I feel I am at my worst or lowest that you see it and love me anyway. I pray for you every day and I know that with everything we have that is good we will pass on to you with hopes that you will plant the seed and make it grow even greater.

John 16:21 (AMP)

A woman, when she is in labor, has pain because her time (to give birth) has come; but when she has given to the child, she no longer remembers the anguish because of her joy that a child has come into the world.

Proverbs 24:3-4 (AMP)

24:3 Through [skillful and Godly] wisdom a house [a life, a home, a family] is built, and by understanding it is established [on a sound and good foundation], 24:4 And by knowledge its rooms are filled with all precious and pleasant riches

Tables Of Content

Preface..1
Know/Love Thyself...4
Who Is He/She?...13
Religion...21
Finances...25
Sex...33
Communication/Pillowtalk..............................40
Dating...48
Travel..56
Health...58
Children/Family Planning................................63
Job, Self-Employed, or Both 77
Family Members & Friends 80
Goal Setting...91
Marriage...94
Goal Your Way..103

Preface

During Covid-19 (it's still going on) I heard so many people talking about divorce. It really hurt my heart that during this time so many could not stand to be in the same space with their spouse or their children. I felt compelled to share some very helpful information that I wished someone had shared with me. I am not a doctor, psychologist, or licensed in any way to treat anyone but I do have my own life experience. Everyone has a story and the best thing to do is get in formation so you are prepared for what is to come.

It is my hope that this informative read will help others to see some important things that they may not have been able to see due to being so busy with work or kids. Both my husband and I had been divorced prior and have shared some things that we had in common. The way that you comprehend when you're younger is way different than when you get older. You live and you learn. Life can teach you some real lessons while at the same time, time will teach and heal a lot of wounds. If you are willing to hear or do the work this may help anyone that is married, single, divorced, widowed, or in a relationship contemplating marriage.

Matthew 11:15 (AMP)

He who has ears to hear, let him hear.

Mark 4:8 (MSG)

3-8 "Listen. What do you make of this? A farmer planted seed. As he scattered the seed, some of it fell on the road and birds ate it. Some fell in the gravel; it

sprouted quickly but didn't put down roots, so when the sun came up it withered just as quickly. Some fell in the weeds; as it came up, it was strangled among the weeds and nothing came of it. Some fell on good earth and came up with a flourish, producing a harvest exceeding his wildest dreams.

I Corinthians 13: (AMP)

1 If I speak with the tongues of men and of angels, but have not love [for others growing out of God's love for me], then I have become only a noisy gong or a clanging cymbal [just an annoying distraction]. 2 And if I have the gift of prophecy [and speak a new message from God to the people], and understand all mysteries, and [possess] all knowledge; and if I have all [sufficient] faith so that I can remove mountains, but do not have love [reaching out to others], I am nothing. 3 If I give all my possessions to feed the poor, and if I surrender my body to be burned, but do not have love, it does me no good at all.

4 Love endures with patience and serenity, love is kind and thoughtful, and is not jealous or envious; love does not brag and is not proud or arrogant. 5 It is not rude; it is not self-

seeking, it is not provoked [nor overly sensitive and easily angered]; it does not take into account a wrong endured. 6 It does not rejoice at injustice, but rejoices with the truth [when right and truth prevail]. 7 Love bears all things [regardless of what comes], believes all things [looking for the best in each one], hopes all things [remaining steadfast during difficult times], endures all things [without weakening].

8 Love never fails [it never fades nor ends]. But as for prophecies, they will pass away; as for tongues, they will cease; as for the gift of special knowledge, it will pass away. 9 For we know in part, and we prophesy in part [for our knowledge is fragmentary and incomplete]. 10 But when that which is complete and perfect comes, that which is incomplete and partial will pass away.

Know / Love Thyself

Psalm 139: 13-14 (NIV)

139:13 For you created my inmost being; you knit me together in my mother's womb. 139:14 I praise you because I am fearfully and wonderfully made: your works are wonderful; I know that full well.

We always have certain things that we require from someone else but it is so important that we require things from ourselves. Sometimes we get caught up in the timeline of the way we think things should go or we are so busy watching someone else's life. You have to be patient with yourself and realize that even you need time to develop. When having conversations with our family or friends we know what we want and we expect this person to be all those things and then some. We fail to ask ourselves some questions.

In our journey of exploring who we are as individuals one must ask the famous questions:

*Are you all those things that you require from someone else?

*Have you prepared yourself to be you and to be you with someone else?

A lot of people are self-absorbed with their egotism and only put the effort into dissecting others to maintain the idea that there is nothing unsuitable about them. They may not be audacious enough to adduce those things that are inside because it may make them feel inadequate. You have to realize that it is so much of the opposite. Who is there to judge you while you work on yourself? Facing those things that are incumbent on your soul. It is just you giving yourself the criticism that you need to work on things. It's a health check. You need to make sure you are not still eating baby food when you should be eating a full course meal.

When you are in a relationship with someone sometimes the way that we do things will be challenged or even the way that you think. Are you prepared for that? Being able to submit to someone doesn't mean changing everything that you are. It means to still be you (the person that they love) and allow space for additional information to be added to you. It's like taking 2-chapter books and putting them together. When you put those together, you continue together writing the rest of your story.

Before you can get to know someone in their 4 seasons you need to know yourself in those same seasons to see how you will react or should I say respond (there is a difference). How are you when the bills are due and you don't have the money to pay them? How are you when everything is all good and there is more than enough? How do you move when there is just enough? How are you when you have lost it all and you have to start over (a lot of people are doing this right now during Covid-19)? Are you willing to recreate yourself when God shows you that it is time for a change? You know when that well starts to run dry because you didn't move when you were supposed to and now you are in a bind. Who do you become when your back is against the wall?

Ask yourself:

- Who are you, what makes you laugh?
- Can you cook and clean? What is clean to you?
- Where would you like to travel?

- What do you enjoy reading?
- What are those parts of you that still need healing (break-ups, childhood, failures)?
- What makes you feel good, what are triggers for you (things that automatically make you react, whether good or bad)?
- Do you like to go out (club, live music, riding through the city, eating out), what pulls your attention?
- What type of music do you like?
- What makes your soul smile? What food do you like?
- What is your purpose? What are your goals?
- Do you know how to treat yourself?
- Have you learned how to take care of yourself (on your own)?
- What have you accomplished just for yourself?
- What are your boundaries? Your definite No's?
- What do you do for yourself that makes you feel good? (nails, hair, make-up, bubble baths, haircuts, taking yourself to dinner)?
- Do you have any addictions that you need to take care of?
- Do you eat well, have fitness goals, and health check-ups (do you take care of yourself)?

- Do you make coherent decisions?
- Are you consistent in what you do?
- Are you a narcissist?

It is so important to know who you are before you enter into a serious relationship. To make sure that you have fallen in love with every flaw and all those things that make you who you are. I can tell you that when you get married young it is so hard to find out who you are separate from someone else. People do it every day so I have nothing against it but for me it was difficult. You don't even know what it's like to accomplish anything on your own. That feeling of paying your bills and providing for yourself away from home. Building your strength and having to account for your own mistakes takes some time and work.

When you get married young, you have not given yourself the chance to breathe and see what road you will take. You may need to go down that road several times before you get what you need. I know some will say that I am wrong but I am totally fine with that. To each his own. For me, I believe you need time to grow up. I mean past college too. Some people say college made them ready. No. College doesn't make you ready for marriage. It helps you discover different career paths to take to financially support yourself. It does not show you how to add a person to your life or take care of yourself.

After marriage, you are so busy with your life happening that you have no time to discover you only what you guys are together. Most days you are so busy taking care of everyone else that you become last on the list. I tell you what though when you know who you are it changes how you respond to others and even with your day being full you are left fulfilled and satisfied. The independent you will tell a person in a minute, "I got this." I don't need any help and if you leave me hey God will bring someone else. Well, guess what this is true but how will you make room for the other person to feel like you need them. I remember feeling like that when I was making it happen for my kids.

QUICK STORY:

Getting to Know Me

After my divorce, I realized that it was the first time in my life that I had been really on my own. I mean besides the fact that I had 4 children along with me; it was the first time I was alone. I looked in the mirror at myself and realized that I hadn't looked at myself since high school. I mean looked at just me and wondered what I was going to do next. I looked and wondered who I was. I realized that I had so much work to do me. Life had been really tough and I needed some time to breathe. Then it hit me.

This is about to be hard.

The realization that I knew very little about myself but that I was going to have to learn about myself to teach my children. I knew that I needed to heal some wombs that were pouring out from the inside. Things that I had buried and left there for years started to surface. I thought I could just leave it there and move on. Now that I had the time to think and see myself, that mirror didn't look so good. You want to talk about a moment where you have to walk something out. While working 50-70 hours a week and taking care of 4 children, I had no idea how I was going to do this. I decided that no matter what, I wasn't going to waste this moment. I wasn't running from my past or trying so hard to make someone love me. I was going to learn to love myself. I had to work hard at making myself love myself. I had to let go of the mask that I used to smile even when I was just falling apart on the inside. I was learning to laugh when I wanted to and how I wanted to without someone looking at me crazy. Oh yeah, and if they did, I didn't care. I would cry if I needed to or talk when I needed and my goal was to be well. I went to counseling at my old church. I went from crying the first day to smiling on my last day. I wanted to know myself and love myself so that I could walk with my head up. God had placed me on the potter's wheel and was shaping me to be Custom made. I didn't want my children to be just like me but better.

How would they be better?

I didn't want to use my kids to make up for what I didn't have or what I didn't get to do. I wanted to raise them right and give them a chance to see things but not through my pain. I knew every ounce of where I came from and what I had been through had come at a cost that I had already paid with time. I was finding my strength. My peace of mind. I was smiling again. My kids were well and taken care of. I was proud of myself. I worked hard and I felt accomplished. I was loving myself for what I was and what I wasn't. Once all that happened, I met my Love. My King. My Baby. My Honey. You know. My all that and then some.

Now, this is where knowing who you are and loving yourself shows some of its importance....

Once I met my Love, I began to wonder what he needed me for. He had it all. A business, a car, he loved himself, he dressed well, he was spiritually together, he traveled, and everything else. Okay, that's great but you want to know what he didn't have. Me! I wasn't there. I had so much to add to him other than sex. I added love, compassion, laughter, prayer partner, the ability to add to the business, someone to share things with, to go places with, to run ideas by. You know that saying that 2 heads are better than 1. That kind of addition. If I failed or he failed we had each other's back. His experience and mine together made for a pretty hefty table to sit down and eat. I'm a full person over here with all kinds of things to offer. Let's not forget I am an earthquake by myself but with him, I am a tidal wave. I can shake it but together we make moves with power. It may not be your moves but it's ours. In our home, he is the King and I am the Queen.

Knowing who I am is very important. Knowing my power and my ability to be stretched matters. Loving who I am is vital to my existence. You have to constantly examine yourself and see what needs to be grown.

Cultivate your gifts that God blessed you with.

DAILY AFFIRMATIONS:

- I am favored, strong, lobed, creative, intelligent, a communicator, healthy, spiritually connected, and I inspire myself

- I have hopes and dreams that are being fulfilled. I can do this.

- I am positive and I give out great positive energy.

- I am going to meet people that will plant good seed into my life.

- I can do all things through Christ who strengthens me.

- I have faith greater than a mustard seed.

- God believes in me and so do I believe in myself

- I have more than enough to be a blessing to others.

- My cup runneth over with great things.

- I am not a victim but I am courageous and victorious.

- My platform is being expanded.

Stay current with yourself and always building.

Who is He/She?

Matthew 25:12 (AMP)

But He replied, "I assure you and most solemnly say to you, I do not know you [we have no relationship].

Psalm 85:10 (AMP)

Steadfast love and truth and faithfulness meet together, Righteousness and peace kiss each other

This is so important because you need to know who you are connecting yourself to. You should never be afraid to ask a question and if you are then you are not ready to be in a relationship with someone. You will be surprised about some things but there should not be any major surprises. Let's also be honest, you will not know everything. Check out a person's social media and what they posted before meeting you. Get to know family and friends. Don't be afraid of the answer because that is a gift to you. After you ask, Listen. Don't just listen so you can ask the next question. Listen clearly so you have a real understanding of what someone is really trying to say to you. You must ask questions and any that you don't ask is totally on you. We always tell our children: Every question asked gets you closer to your understanding and it doesn't matter what the question is, it is not dumb. It is better to have asked once than to have never asked at all.

ASK QUESTIONS!!! If you don't know what to ask, I have some right here:

- What do you enjoy doing in your spare time?
- Where is your favorite place to travel?
- What is your favorite type of movie, tv-show, or sports team (plans for future dates)?
- What is your favorite color (you may want to buy them something nice)?

- What is your favorite restaurant and type of food)?

- Do you go to strip clubs (why and how often)?

- How would you describe yourself to me if you have to write an essay about who you are?

- Do you smoke, drink, or do drugs? (any prior addictions even to sex)?

- Do you have a criminal record? What is it and when did this offense occur?

- What are your political views?

- Do you like to exercise? How often?

- What do you like to do to stay healthy physically, mentally, and spiritually? (dating opportunity)

- Have you ever been tested for Aids or had an STD? How long ago?

- Did you finish school? What Level? If not, Why?

- What do you do for a living? How long have you done this and are you still currently doing it?

- What are your goals? Where do you see yourself in the next 5 years? How will you accomplish these goals?

- When was your last relationship? What did you learn from it? Have you healed from whatever caused it to end?

- Is there anything that you feel you need to work on? (someone should always be looking for ways to grow)

- Who do you consider to be your support system or your circle?

- Do you have siblings? How many? How is your relationship?

- Where are you from (not Venus or Mars, what state have you lived in most of your life, where were you born)

- Who are your parents and where did they come from? Are your parents married or divorced? How long? How is your relationship with your parents?

- Do you have any health disorders that are hereditary (for your spouse and future children)?

- Do you have any close friends? Are they the same sex or opposite (this could be a deal-breaker for some)? How long have you known your friends? Have you ever had sex with any of your friends? How often do you guys go out?

- What do you do when you go out? Have you ever had a relationship with the same sex?

- Have you always identified as a male or female?

- Do you have any children? How many? Do they live with you or the other parent? How do you get to spend time with them? Are they okay having a new person in their life or is it too soon? If not, how many kids would you like to have?

- How do you handle financial responsibility?

- How is your credit?

- Do you live on your own, with your parents, a roommate, or with friends?

- Do you hope to get married one day (the reason for a relationship is not just to go out-depends on the person)?

- What does marriage mean to you?

I believe that it is so important to know if a person believes that a relationship means multiple people or just us. Maybe it could mean opportunistic or just for the moment. All of these questions are great conversation pieces. Things that you should know before you get married. If you have already gotten married then these are questions that are still important. You should know about the health of your spouse for the sake of your family. Remember when someone is telling you about themselves that you have to pay attention to more than just their words. The more that you are around them you will be able to watch facial expressions, body language, and habits.

People can only hide their true selves for so long. Pay attention. Listen and learn. This is not just to see if they are who they say they are but so you can surprise them and do special things that they may enjoy. Once you know what they enjoy then you can add some zest to spice it up.

DON'T EXCLUDE

On another note, don't exclude someone because they don't know what you know. They may not be a college graduate but they may know how to put some things together. You may be able to drive the car but they know what to do to make that car drivable if you know what I mean.

When you introduce something new to them, allow them to try to hear you and learn. They may not have been exposed to things like that or it may not have crossed their mind. Once you have introduced the idea and had the opportunity to share and teach that will let you know if a person is willing to try new things or take interest in what you know. Then too, that just may not be their cup of tea (after they have tried to get the information).

Don't get stuck on someone having potential although that is a start but see if they are self-motivated to make things happen. Not just for you guys but in making major decisions that are life-altering for themselves. The exclusion doesn't just mean education or money but also in the way a person looks. He or she may be a little overweight. Go to the gym, body suits, and so much more is out here. Their hair may not be the way you want it. Wigs, braids, extensions, dye, haircuts, and once again everything else. Those are all minor things. You want what's behind all that. The heart of the person. Divorces or the end of all relationships don't just come from looks or money. It comes from the heart. Not being heard.

QUICK STORY:

My husband and I had to learn about each other with limited time. Most of our conversations had to take place on the phone, facetime, when I could get a moment from work, overnight while the kids slept, or when he came off the road. It was crazy trying to learn from each other under the circumstances. Dating was hard because I rarely had anyone to keep the kids and when they did, they didn't want to. We still worked hard to find out what we could. Once we established our relationship and he finally got a chance to meet the kids it got better. We were finally able to spend some time together. He got a chance to get to know me even in my weakest moments and I got a chance to do the same with him. During our journey, we knew that it would just take some time. (You will find out more about this later on in the book to see what you can do to get creative!)

Let time have its moment. What you find perplexing and the most aggravating as you get to know each other will either be a deal-breaker or something you will laugh at later.

Proverbs 18:2 (AMP)

A [closed-minded] fool does not delight in understanding, But only in revealing his personal opinions [unwittingly displaying his self-indulgence and his stupidity].

Religion

James 1:26-27 (MSG)

Anyone who sets himself up as "religious" by talking a good game is self-deceived. This kind of religion is hot air and only hot air. Real religion, the kind that passes muster before God the Father, is this: Reach out to the homeless and loveless in their plight and guard against corruption from the godless world.

People always assume that because two people are together that they both believe the same. That is not always the case. It has been found that having a certain religion that does not appeal to the other can cause a major disruption in the household. There has to be a bond built around this center of all relationships. You have to be able to agree on how you would like to pray together or alone and even so much as raise your children. It may seem okay in the beginning that one has such a difference but when there are additions such as children you have to decide how you will introduce your ever so loving relationship with your Creator to your children.

ASK EACHOTHER:

- Do you share the same belief?

- Does it matter if you go to church or view online? If you decide not to attend how would that make the other feel? How will you bond over this matter?

- How will you continue to connect to your center although it may differ from your significant other?

- If you attend a physical setting, where will it be?

- Is it enough to know that at the end of the day we all know that there is One God which is our Creator or is it more important on how you live in worship? Meaning, how you pray, what you wear, the book of spiritual guidance (Holy Bible, Bhagavata Purana, Upanishads, Veda, Guru

Granth Sahib, Tripitaka-Dhammapada, The Holy Quran, Torah, Talmud, Kitab-I-Aqdas, The Agamas, Kojiki, and much more).

ASK YOURSELF:

- What are your religious beliefs? Were you raised in a household that practiced this? Are you willing to convert? If you are willing to convert, how will that affect you and your inner being? Will it cause a split between you and your family?

- Are you willing to sacrifice your relationship with friends and family? How will you move forward from this?

- Would your family accept the person that you decide to marry if they don't share their same beliefs (this is huge in some families)?

Can you survive this?

Most couples can survive this because they have mutual respect for the other and their beliefs. They realize that they don't have the power to change someone but to show them who they are not just by what they believe but by how they treat someone. Your audio matches your video (like the movies that are in a different language but they change it over to the language of your choice. Remember that this should not lead to you hurting someone because they were raised to believe a certain way. If you have chosen your belief that they have that same right.

QUICK STORY:

The funniest thing happened with my husband and me when we were getting to know each other. We were talking about something about religion. I remember saying, "I am with Jesus and I don't care what anyone says. He wondered had he offended me by talking about other religions and where they derived from. He said; "Hey I love God too and I know who He is to me." We laughed but it was at that moment I realized how immature I was. I had lacked exposure to any other religion and I had never considered the fact that I would come across so many people that loved God but worshipped Him differently.

I started to meet people from different countries and find that they were connected to God in their way and that they believed in His power. It was amazing. I was able to continue in my relationship with my Creator but also stand next to my fellow brother and sister without criticism in my heart. Learning this made me love more and develop a greater respect for others and their journey.

Jeremiah 31:3 (NIV)

The Lord hath appeared of old unto me, saying, Yea, I have loved thee with an everlasting love: therefore, with lovingkindness have I drawn thee.

Finances

Proverbs 24:27 (AMP)

Prepare your work outside And get it ready for yourself in the field; Afterward, build your house and establish a home.

Proverbs 21:5 (AMP)

The plans of the diligent lead surely to abundance and advantage, But everyone who acts in haste comes surely to poverty.

Proverbs 13:16 (AMP)

Every prudent and self-disciplined man acts with knowledge, But a [closed-minded] fool [who refuses to learn] displays his foolishness [for all to see].

Proverbs 30:24-25 (AMP)

24There are four things that are small on the earth, But they are exceedingly wise: 25The ants are not a strong people, Yet they prepare their food in the summer

Proverbs 22:7 (AMP)

The rich rule over the poor And the borrower is servant to the lender.

Luke 14:28-30 (AMP)

28 For which one of you, when he wants to build a watchtower [for his guards], does not first sit down and calculate the cost, to see if he has enough to finish it? 29 Otherwise, when he has laid a foundation and is unable to finish [the building], all who see it will begin to ridicule him, 30 saying, 'This man began to build and was not able to finish!'

Ecclesiastes 11:2-6 (NIV)

2 Invest in seven ventures, yes, in eight; you do not know what disaster may come upon the land. 3 If clouds are full of water, they pour rain on the earth. Whether a tree falls to the south or to the north, in the place where it falls, there it will lie. 4 Whoever watches the wind will not plant; whoever looks at the clouds will not reap. 5 As you do not know the path of the wind, or how the body is formed in a mother's womb, so you cannot understand the work of God, the Maker of all things. 6 Sow your seed in the morning, and at evening let your hands not be idle, for you do not know which will succeed, whether this or that, or whether both will do equally well.

This has been a key factor in several relationships coming to an end. It causes arguments, frustration, suicide, loss of homes and cars, and many other things. Also, there are good things that go along with it. Families flourish, vacation, start business', buy homes and cars, retire, invest, and once again so much more.

A lot of people don't want to talk about it. They feel like you are invading their privacy. The truth is you are. Your privacy together. Why would you not want your spouse to know where you stand together? It may be embarrassing or hard to deal with but once you put it out there you can work on it. You are an addition to each other. One may know a little more than the other.

Don't just talk to each other; talk to your children. Let them know what it's all about so they have a leg to stand on. Don't make them think that it is a walk in the park. Tell them how much work you had to do or what your parents had to do to make sure you were taken care of. We don't want our children thinking that they can just get everything for free. Nothing is free. All things come at a cost even if it's our time. Every household whether single or married has a certain way that they talk about finances. To each his own.

I remember my parents saying this is my money and that is your money. They would assign bills and if one needed more money then they would loan it to them and say you have to pay me back. I never understood that. So, I knew that would not work for me. I felt like once I got married it would be our money together and the bills all come out of a joint account. It didn't matter to me who made the most money because we were both building something together. I heard people talking about prenuptial agreements. Once again; do you, whatever that is. If that is what you feel like you need to do then that is on you and the person you are with.

There are people in this world who may have some bad intentions. I feel like when God has something for you it will be yours and whatever is lost will come again. Most times it comes back greater than before. My husband keeps. There is not a just-in-case or a plan in place for someone to leave.

LET'S TALK ABOUT IT:

- Credit cards and loans
- Student loans
- Stocks and Investments
- Retirement (401(k), 403(b), Roth IRA, Individual Retirement Arrangements (IRAs), Simple IRA Plans (savings incentive match plans for employees), Payroll Deduction IRAs, SEP Plans (Simplified Employee Pension, SARSEP Plans (Salary Reduction Simplified Employee Pension),
- Profit-Sharing Plans, Employee Stock Ownership Plans (ESOPs), Money Purchase Plans, Defined Benefit Plans
- Debt of any kind
- Budgets

- Other sources of income
- Savings (Do you have any, how much, and what is the goal together)
- Bank Accounts (Yours, Mine, Ours?) What Bank?
- Shopping (personal, household, grocery)
- Home (Rent or Mortgage)
- Day care or Private School
- Vehicles (Cash Car or Monthly Payment)
- Insurance (Medical, Dental, Vehicle, Rental, Life) [traffic violations, location, and poor health will cause the prices of these to increase]
- Bankruptcy
- Entrepreneurship. What is the overhead cost of running your own business? Are you taking a loss or making a profit? Taxes.

QUICK STORY:

I know this has to be a very important topic because growing up we stayed in a neighborhood that was income-based and definitely had to get subsidies to make ends meet (WIC, food-stamps, Medicaid, utility checks, free rent, and anything else they had to offer). My parents never talked to me about money. Not even so much as sat down and showed me what it takes to pay the bills. I remember our family being completely dependent on family members and the church. I paid close attention to everything they did. I think because our lives were so hard that I decided to be different. I saw they worked at a carwash so I asked to work there too. I asked the owner and he let me work there for a little while. I was about 11 years old at the time. Around 14 I went through a work program and got approved to work at a couple of places for the summer. That kept me out of trouble and making money. Then I finally landed my first job. I was able to get my first car by my grandad co-signing for me. I paid my car note, car insurance, phone bill, and helped my parents with bills and their car too. Mind you, I was still in high school. I was very proud of myself. I did all that because I didn't want to end up living like we were. I wanted to show myself that I could take care of myself. It's one thing to be able to take care of yourself but it is a different story when someone else joins the team and even more so when little ones join.

You need to have a very healthy sense of where you are and where you plan to go. Work together and see what needs to be done. Come up with a plan. When someone says that they pay their bills ask them; How often? Their idea might be to pay the least amount due before they are disconnected. It's never too late to have these conversations. Make time for them. This is not just at the beginning of a relationship. You have to do this every week or once a month.

Life has a way of changing how you do things so make sure you try your best to be ready.

*Throughout this short book you will find more financial conversations to have as well as discover what causes a shift.

Sex...
Hebrews 13:4

Let marriage be held in honor among all, and let the marriage bed be undefiled, for God will judge the sexual immoral and adulteress

I know in most churches and other places that we go for spiritual uplifting that this subject is never really spoken of. It's like this silent subject that no one wants to talk about. This is strange because so many relationships have ended because of unfulfillment or being ashamed of feeling provocative. People are so different in the way they are taught how to think or feel about sex. Some people say it's not a priority, that it's wrong to even think of it until you reach a certain age or even until marriage. Fact check, these things do cross your mind and it is so important to be educated. We hear don't cheat or before marriage don't fornicate, and save yourself for marriage. While all being great things it can also leave someone with an unhealthy expectation of what sex is.

Get educated and have some conversations.

ASK QUESTIONS!!!

Has anyone ever just walked up to you and hit you with something? Most of you are like, no or you know exactly what I'm talking about. If you have then you know it doesn't feel good to have someone just do something like that to you. Well, imagine not having any information and going into the room with your husband or wife for the first time and he or she does something that just completely turns you off. I mean it just leaves you with a fear of ever being vulnerable again. How about you walk in a room only to see your spouse has all kinds of toys and you start to feel like you are not satisfying them and wonder where everything went wrong or are you doing this with me because you are thinking of someone else? This is why it is important to talk about this.

Maybe you are a virgin and your spouse isn't. Explore. It's not meant to be painful unless you're into that but all in all, it's pure pleasure and the ability to become one with your soul mate. This is the space in your relationship where not only are you emotionally naked but you are physically naked baring everything.

Song of Songs 7:7-10

"Your stature is like that of the palm, and your breast like clusters of fruit. I said, 'I will climb the palm tree; I will take hold of its fruit.' May your breast be like clusters of grapes on the vine, the fragrance of your breath like apples, and your mouth like the best wine. May the wine go straight to my beloved, flowing gently over lips and teeth. I belong to my beloved, and his desire is for me."

The Bible is about teaching lessons, right. Okay well, let's get to the lesson that will have you blushing. Sex is not just a physical connection but a spiritual connection that you have once you partake in this very passionate event. Yes, I called it an event. Why? Well, it should be fun, pleasurable, put a smile in places that no one knows but you and your spouse, and it should leave you satisfied but yet longing for the next one. To have that thought in the back of your mind; I can't wait to get my hands, legs, lips, arms, and whatever else on you. Do you know how much of a turn-on it is to know that you don't have to worry about a disease or even the thought of someone touching what's yours? You can try anything and do anything you want without anyone else knowing your business and forming their opinion of you. Just you and your boo. There should be all kinds of good trouble you can get into.

Buy lingerie and surprise each other. Call your spouse to the room and just surprise them. Show up to their job and take them to lunch but let the lunch be at the hotel close by. Sex is also a great way to relieve stress. Try it. My husband and I were talking about sex and what we have heard or read (a great thing to do with your spouse). Often we talk about how important it is to connect with each other. We laughed at the words exchanged, "We might be mad at each other about something but that situation has nothing to do with our desire to have sex with each other.

Most people believe that all sex is the same or they are left feeling unfulfilled after. Well, there is a connection that you have that changes everything besides all the positions that you can do with someone. It's something about that connection that changes the entire flow of things. Passion. Desire. Romance. Trust. Anyone can just have sex but when you have it with that special person in your life it changes its meaning. What my husband and I do is private and that's just that. I don't share details or any of those things with anyone. Besides no one needs to know your most intimate details.

ASK THE QUESTION:

- What do you like? How do you like to be touched? Where is your G-Spot? Where is your hot spot?

- What lights up your fire? Is it romance, dinner, comedy, or drinks?

- What is your favorite angle? Do I like it anytime (morning, noon, night which includes in the middle of the night)?

- Am I okay with having sex with my menstrual cycle on (some people call this going to war)? Say it's nasty, gross, or even unsanitary but this does happen between some people.

Now, let's go even deeper.

WHAT DO YOU LIKE:

- to be spanked (hard or soft)
- oral sex or anal sex
- pearl necklaces
- hand jobs (fast or slow)
- quickies
- hand cuffs, blind folds, and whips
- cowgirl (don't be scared, you have control here) doggy style, missionary, lazy dog, and many more to choose from
- throwing it back

- on the wall, the couch, the bed, the floor, in the car, shower, tub, garage, outside, and where ever else
- stripper pole, swings, toys, and games
- loud with moaning or quiet
- Naked or Lingerie

Too much....

Well, listen up. This is reality. You are a human being and you require what you require. Let's not get shy when it comes down to the person you are spending your entire life with. They deserve all of you. Every thought and every opportunity to please every part of you. Why not immerse and indulge with the sexiest, hypnotic, fascinating, being that God created just for you? How can you truly open yourself up to being with someone if you can't be honest about what you desire? Step outside of what someone taught you and learn from each other. Build your own sexual connection with each other. It is like kinetic sand that continuously gravitates to every part or like water in the ocean that never separates but only moves to the motions of the wind creating waves and earth's natural changes that causes you to evolve because of its massiveness (you are the wind and you are the earth's natural change).

Knock each other's socks off!!!

Blow each other's minds!!!

Communication/Pillowtalk

James 2:17 (AMP)

So also faith, if it does not have works (deeds and actions of to back it up), by itself is destitute of power (inoperative, dead).

This is the most important thing in your relationship to remember. Before you touch my body, you touch my mind. You touch my very soul with the depth of your words which ignites my spirit and causes our lives to become intertwined.

Whomever you have chosen to be connected to should know your innermost secrets. You may have one of your really big ideas even if it seems impossible to you, your spouse will be the one that is most honest and will push you to go for it. There are so many forms of communication: Talking, touching, listening, watching, writing, and so much more Notice all those forms of communication require an action.

When things get hard it is not time to retreat. It's time to talk. Time to communicate. One thing people try to do is avoid. Avoid each other when they are hurt or angry. One of the thoughts is, I will just pray. I love to pray with my husband but I also love to have my personal prayer. Now let's be clear, it is so important to be connected to our Creator and know that He can do all things. I don't doubt the power of my Creator. So, with that being said I need to enlighten you on the work that you are going to have to do to grow your relationship. Why would I say something like that? Well, I was taught that all I had to do was pray about it and God would fix it. Just call on Him and He will take care of it. Let me tell you this: That is like saying I hope my spouse knows that I am so very proud of them. How? You have to get up and go tell them how proud of them you are.

Communication is the key. It is the key to the very heart of each other.

QUICK STORY:

When my husband and I got married we had our children there and an attorney. He gave us some information that most don't. He said be careful what you say to each other because those words stick with you and it takes a while to heal. So, when you get angry walk away until you calm down. He was so right. It's easy to put those words out there because you're angry and it's making you feel better but what you can't see is every word is a brick that builds a wall. You have no idea what type of wall because it contains so many bricks. It could be filled with mistrust, unappreciation, resentment, and so many other things. Just as quick as you tore it down it will take so much more to build it back up. Be careful. It's hard to trust someone with your feelings if you share them with that person and they ignore, get angry, or make you feel like you are wrong for having feelings. It will save you a lot of tears and time if you handle learn what is effective or ineffective communication.

Do not use sex as a way to communicate how angry you are with someone. Meaning with holding sex because you are mad about something someone did or said. It's not for that. Some people have make-up sex as a form to communicate that everything is fine. Sex does not fix the problem. It only soothes the problem for the moment. You will revisit the same problem that you had before your desire to touch your spouse. Just because you got mad didn't mean that they physically became unattractive it just means you were not attracted to their words at the moment and how they made you feel.

James 1:19 (AMP)

Understand this, my beloved brothers and sisters. Let everyone be quick to hear (be a careful, thoughtful listener), slow to speak (a speaker of carefully chosen words and), slow to anger (patient, reflective, forgiving)

Proverbs 25:11 (AMP)

A word fitly spoken is like apples of gold in a setting of silver.

Proverbs 15:1 (AMP)

A soft answer turns away wrath, but a harsh word stirs up anger

Proverbs 18:21 (AMP)

Death and life are in the power of the tongue, and those who love it will eat its fruits

Proverbs 15:4 (AMP)

A gentle tongue is a tree of life, but perverseness in it breaks the spirit I could go on and on but this is necessary.

How do you effectively communicate? First of all, be yourself. Don't be afraid of someone else's response. Say what you need to say. If you feel a certain way you need to say it so that you both have an understanding of where you are. You have to keep your eyes on the person so you can see their facial expression, listen very carefully, and ask questions. It doesn't matter what the question is make sure you get an understanding of what your spouse is saying. You may not have a response right away and that's okay. That's why you are in a relationship, you can always revisit that conversation. Don't overtalk each other. I was told that when someone is talking and you start to talk, it takes away the value of what you have to say because they can't hear what you are really trying to communicate to them. Place yourself in the other person's shoes often. This helps you to try to understand how they are feeling and why they are saying what they are saying. If you are listening to respond then there is a problem with your communication already. You are not totally hearing the special person in your life. If you know the what and not the why then how will you get to the bottom of what is causing those feelings to arise. Communication helps you to know when it's time to talk to someone and when to patiently wait. It helps you get to know someone.

Remember that first thing you said to your spouse. I mean the very first time you met and exchanged words. That very first phone call, inbox, text message, snap chat, or direct message. Remember how much you wanted to make each other smile or want the other to desire you more. You couldn't wait until the next time you got to talk. You would talk all night on the phone or write letters. Drop off roses just to put a smile on their face. Stop by just to take them to lunch while they are at work. If you got angry you wouldn't dare try to offend the other because you didn't want to lose them. Then as time went on you kept communicating and finally got comfortable saying a little more. So, now you are finally beginning to communicate. You got past the introduction and now you are getting to know who you are together and how that is going to work.

Communicate about everything. How was your day, what happened at work, did you meet any new people, how are you feeling, and any other things that you want to talk about? What happened with the kids, did you find that jacket that you were looking for, or how is your family doing today? Hey, can we sit down and look at the bills, I was thinking about starting a new business, or I felt so upset when you told me...Bottom line you are not just connected by your body or spirit. You are also trying to stay on the same page with each other.

Have you ever been sitting right next to your spouse and you guys were thinking the same thing? Maybe you looked at each other from across the room and knew exactly what you guys were smiling about or if you were ready to go. Connected. Remember that all communication is not about what went wrong. It's also about what went right. Tell how happy something made you feel or how turned on you were when your spouse did this or that. Say you did a good job Love and I appreciate you. Tell it all. Tell jokes even if it is corny. Who better to be corny with?

Be an open book!!!

Everyone has not been raised to communicate like you. Some people are raised around a lot of chaos (yelling, hitting, cursing). Be very careful with this type of communicator. You can't predict how someone may respond to you but with this type of communicator, you may want to rethink your situation. Just because someone was raised this way does not mean you deserve to be treated like that. You are a human being. Don't become a victim of this type of behavior. Also, there are observers. They communicate by trying to read your body language. They don't talk much because they don't really know how to. They try to take care of things based on what they think the situation may be. If you don't talk to your spouse you will not know what is really going. If you think for one moment that your face or your feelings alone will tell someone what you mean you are sadly mistaken. You can't just observe you must open your mouth and talk. They work hand and hand.

Observation is for learning.

Talking is for understanding.

Think about this and even if you need classes, learn how to be an effective communicator. Also, remember there is a time and place for all things. You do not want to sit at the table with the kids and talk about your personal relationship or discuss your bills while you are standing in front of the guest. Share your thoughts about what the other is saying and be open to hearing. Don't get angry because the other person is being a person. They have their own way that they see the world and understand it. The only thing you can do is try to help them to see it the way that you have it painted.

People say things differently as well. They may not have the same vocabulary and they are not able to articulate certain things. Sometimes you may be saying the same thing but a different way. It doesn't make either of you wrong. Agree to Disagree. Compromise.

Pillow talk to me is a little different. I try not to have those conversations about the kids, family, or work while we are laying in the bed. Sometimes those conversations happen anyway because the day was full and I still need to talk or he does. However, when you are in bed these are the conversations that you will close your eyes to. Trying to connect after a long day is so important. Take this time to cry if you need to, laugh about some things, and dream together about some things. Maybe talk about vacations, your favorite flowers, your dream car, what you think of each other, or even what your favorite food or date night would be.

Flirt.

Let me say it again, Flirt.

Stay Connected!

Dating

Ephesians 4:3 (AMP)

3 Make every effort to keep the oneness of the Spirit in the bond of peace [each individual working together to make the whole successful].

I Thessalonians 5:11 (AMP)

11 Therefore encourage and comfort one another and build up one another, just as you are doing.

QUICK STORY:

Every time I see the word date, I laugh a little. You may wonder why but I have a couple of reasons. I almost didn't go out on my first date with my husband because I was nervous and scared. I hadn't dated for a very long time. My sister convinced me to go and she helped me pick out an outfit for it. I drove for about an hour or more to get there because I told him that I would much rather drive myself. I got there and was afraid to get out of the car and then when I saw him come around the corner I finally got out. We walked up to the restaurant and lost track of time. We were having such a great time that we didn't even notice everyone had left and they were getting ready to close. Now that's a date.

The other reason I laugh a little is that I remember asking my husband when we first started talking, how he would feel if we couldn't go out on a date. His response was, "What do you mean can't date?" That was one of the most real moments. Let me explain. When he and I met he had a son that was about 20 and I had 4 children that were 10, 6, 6, and 4. I was pretty much doing it by myself while working 50 to 70 hours a week with a little help here and there. So, I wanted him to understand that I didn't have the opportunity to date much and that if he was in the picture it would be very difficult to do so. Now and again we would be able to go out but not like most new couples do. He thought I was joking but soon found out that I was warning him and at the same time letting him know how difficult this would be. We tried our best to date when we could. I know you are probably saying why didn't you just get a sitter. Well, I didn't trust just anyone with my children, I worked a lot of hours, and the help just wasn't there.

I remember us wanting to go out so bad that he offered to pay my mom more money and buy the food for the kids just so we would have someone to watch them so we could spend time together. Understand that we had not gotten to the point where he met the kids yet. My husband was a trooper. He hung in there and so did I. As you can see the word Husband is there. Since you heard a little of our story. I wanted to tell you how important it is to date.

Dating allows you to see each other outside of work, problems, family, and friends. You develop some sort of intimacy. You can openly try new things with each other and build a bond. Maybe drive a go-cart, watch a movie, go out to dinner, cook for each other, dress up or down, work out together, dance, and just do the most romantic or silliest things together. It's almost as if time was just paused and you only have each other to think about. Just because you get married it's not over... Don't think for a moment that when you get married that this is supposed to go away. If anything, it becomes more vital to your relationship.

During your marriage or union, it is your getaway into time and space with each other. Your breath of fresh air. It is so important to set aside time from your busy life to let that "girl" or "guy" know that they still light up your world. They make your heart sing and you wouldn't rather be in any other space than with them.

QUICK STORY:

I remember one time our oldest son had come home and I decided to take my husband out on a date. It had been so long since we had the chance to go. So, I planned it out. At that time, we didn't have a lot of money and so much was going on in our lives that we just had gotten away from the most important reason why we were together. We had forgotten how to date each other. I took him to a bowling alley, we played mini-golf (neither of us had played before), and we went to Krystal's. Not in that order but how the night turned out. Our alley wasn't ready so we headed up to Krystal's to eat. It was there that he and I looked at each other and for a moment there was silence. We had forgotten to laugh. As we ate, we started to talk and finally left to go back and see if it was our time to bowl yet. It still wasn't so we went out to play mini-golf and tried our best to pretend that for that moment it was just us and there were no issues that awaited us. We bowled and headed home.

Our first date after months of not dating. Life had gotten so personal and serious that it just wasn't fun anymore. Mind you that it wasn't because of him and me but there were other things outside of us causing issues. We loved each other dearly and there was not one thought of divorce there. No cheating, no none of that. Just simply allowing time to get away from us. Don't let so much go on that you forget to ask each other out on a date. That you forget that feeling of knowing that it's just you and your spouse in the room.

My husband taught me how to date. I couldn't remember the last time I went out on a real date and felt like I was special until him. He showed me how to step out of the box and try new things, how to laugh again, how to love again, how to trust again, how to connect, that it was okay to enjoy quality things based on the space you are in. He showed me that I was capable of being more, having more, loving more, caring more, and all this from dating.

Before kids, you could just go out when you get ready. After, you have to plan. For us, there were always kids. If you have a sitter, great. If you have parents or siblings, great. If you have a best friend, great. If not, you have got to figure it out. With us, we have 7 children and 6 of them are still at home. Thank God one of them is now old enough to help out but in the meantime, in-between time...we had to get it together.

Get Creative!!!

Don't let money be your way out of dating. No Excuses!!! What are things that you can do at home if you can't go out? Find a series on Netflix, Cable, Hulu, Amazon, Apple tv, or whatever your preference. sit in your bed or on the couch and just binge-watch for hours. We call our garage "Club DuBose". When the kids are watching their movies or go to bed we go in our garage, cut on our music, dance, talk, look on Facebook at the funny post, or whatever we want because it is our time. Cut the grill on, sit outside, pull out those cards, dominos, rush and roulette game, or darts,Take a walk and hold hands, sit down and have a picnic and then walk back home Ride bikes together or be like big kids and jump on the trampoline together Grab your karaoke machine and sing music and listen to some comedy. Maybe just sit on the porch and hold each other Light some candles, put on some music, and eat a very nice meal together. Make a bubble bath with candles and music. Sit in the tub with each other and relax there for a while. Do couples yoga in the living room or your room. Purchase a massage table, handheld electric massager, some body oils. There is a lot to do. No excuses as to why you can't date.

What are things to do if you are heading out on the town?

- If you have 2 cars create a scavenger hunt that leads your spouse to where you are and have a special date planned

- Find a new restaurant each time, some have live music and dancing

- Get couples massages

- Walk trails together

- Drive up to a fast-food place, sit on top of the hill where you can see the view, and eat

- Just hop in the car and drive

- Go fishing

- Sky diving (or indoor sky diving)

- Walk on the beach

- Take a weekend trip (driving or by flight)

- Go shopping together and watch each other try on clothing that you would like to see the other in
- Go skating together, bowling, golfing
- Go to the movies
- Rent or buy some four-wheelers and just go for it together

Once again, there is so much to do. Go online and see what's going on in your area. I will say it again, "NO EXCUSES!!!" Get dressed up and go out. Throw on those hoops and that ponytail or wig that you don't mind getting messed up. Even those heels that stuck in the back of that closet, you won't have them on long anyway. I understand that at home you wear your comfortable clothing but don't forget to let your spouse know that you still want to put something special on just for them (outside of the bedroom). Remind them of that special smell good that you put on. Leave your scent which is settled and not overpowering. Be spontaneous. Keep it spicy.

Date Rules

- Do not use your date time to talk about your problems use this time to bond. Your date is not meant for talking about all of that. You can do that at home. Let it all go so you can enjoy each other. It's a refresher.

- Do not start talking about sad things such as someone being sick or someone who just passed away

- Do not take baggage with you. Meaning leave your anger, resentment, and any other negativity somewhere else. Anywhere else but in this moment.

- Dress for the occasion. It is not cute to have on heels when you are taking a walk or a suit while riding a go-cart. [if your nails, hair, shoes (male and female), or clothing will get in the way of you having fun then don't wear it or fix it differently)

- Don't wait for the other person to ask you out. You can ask too.

Dating pulls your communication and sex altogether

Travel

Psalm 121:7-8 (NIV)

7 The Lord will keep you from all harm—he will watch over your life; 8 the Lord will watch over your coming and going both now and forevermore.

It is so important to plan. If you can plan for work and all these other things. Plan to discover. People always think they can't go to a certain place but if you do your research right you will find there are a whole lot of places you can visit.

THE BIG QUESTIONS ARE:

- Where do you want to go?
- How often would you like to go?
- Who is all going?
- How much will this cost?
- Will it be in the country or out of the country?

This should be so much fun. Discovering what you like to do together, apart, and with family and friends. Imagine you and your spouse on a getaway that is not just full of romance but with bike riding, swimming, dancing, walks on the beach, riding horses, food tasting, comedy, and so much more. Oh, my goodness. So much fun. Now, imagine going out of the country with lots of friends and family. All the fun in the world to have so much laughter, ideas, and people to watch your back.

Traveling is so important because it keeps you from becoming complacent with where you are. Exploring together is vital. You get to see what puts a sparkle in your spouse's interest and yours. Try it. Come together on a place, plan for it, go, and see what happens next.

Health

3 John 1:2 (AMP)

Beloved, I pray that in every way you may succeed and prosper and be in good health [physically], just as [I know] your soul prospers [spiritually].

Health is so important. The health of yourself and the people that surround you. When you say you want to spend the rest of your life with someone, what does that mean to you? Would you like to spend it healthy or not well? What about when you say you want to live to see your children do great things or have grandchildren? How about the rest of your life? Would you like to be healthy or does it matter to you? What needs to happen for you to accomplish great health?

LET'S TALK.

I'm not a doctor but I know we have things that we see in our family that pass down to us through our genetics. It's a family thing. Well, there are things that you can do to get in front of it. If you know that high blood pressure or diabetes is prominent in your family, why wait until it happens to you. Go ahead and work out, walk 30 minutes a day, and eat healthily. There may be mental illness in your family that hangs more on disorders but make sure to take time to cater to that area in your life. Do yoga, take walks, dance, get a bike, pilates, meditate, listen to music that is calming to your soul. Look out for each other when it comes down to this. Don't condemn them but help them. Let them know how much you need them and want them around.

Encourage each other to stay healthy.

A lot of times we don't go to the doctor, dentist, or optometrist. We always say we don't have time. Women and men both avoid this because they don't want to deal with the answers that they may get or we just flat out can't afford it. It's better to know than to not know. Can you afford to pass away and your spouse or children are shocked and left with no warning. It does happen to people but why not do everything you can to make sure you are around. Not only do you need to know what's going on but so do your children. For themselves and their children.

ASK YOURSELF:

- What do you know about your health or your spouse's health?

- What about your parents, siblings, or grandparent's health?

- What has happened for them to improve their health?

Let me tell you guys, I had my issues with doctors. I would just put myself off and take everyone else to be seen and never go myself. I had a scare with my blood pressure and I was so afraid of going to sleep. It had gotten so high that all I could do was lay there. Here I am with my husband at work, older kids at school, babies at home with me, and I can't move. My husband called the ambulance and even they couldn't believe it. This is what we don't think about. I don't know about you but I look forward to a long life. I not only want it to live long but I want to live healthily and enjoy my full life.

There are things that even in the best shape happen to people. Make sure you have the proper insurance or financial means to take care of each other.

ASK YOURSELF:

- Are you prepared to take care of your spouse in the case that they become incapacitated?
- Are you able to take care of your spouse in the case of an unexpected illness?
- Do you have life insurance or a will?

Please, please, please make sure you discuss death. I know we don't want to talk about it but you must. This happens even though we don't want it to. My husband and I had a hard time talking about it. It is difficult to imagine yourself passing away. I tear up with just the thought of my family moving forward without me. Not being able to kiss them, hug them, talk to them, and all that goes with love. To be honest you have to see it differently. How can you love them and leave them with major debt? How can you not discuss the major effect that death will have on your family? Let's face this head-on. One day we will pass away, we just don't know when.

FIND OUT ABOUT OR HAVE AN IDEA:

- Burial plots
- Funeral Arrangements
- Locations

Set time aside to take care of yourself.

Children/Family Planning

Proverbs 22:6 AMP

Train up a child in the way he should go [teaching him to seek God's wisdom and will for his abilities and talents], Even when he is old, he will not depart from it.

Psalms 127:3 AMP

Behold, children are a heritage and gift from the LORD, The fruit of the womb a reward.

John 16:21 (AMP)

21 A woman, when she is in labor, has pain because her time [to give birth] has come; but when she has given birth to the child, she no longer remembers the anguish because of her joy that a child has come into the world.

Children are such a blessing. When your Creator entrusts you to carry a soul and bring this wonderful soul into this world...He must think the world of you. It's nothing easy about it. The very work that goes into carrying this life inside your body is nothing less than angelic. How the body is formed, every cell, the nervous system, the brain, the heart, every feature, toes, fingers, the eyes, the spine, and everything else. Knowing that they are connected to our bodies through an umbilical cord that supplies nutrients and oxygen to our little one or ones. Then the day comes where they finally arrive into this world and even more, now you have a full responsibility to train, teach, discipline, protect, take care of financially, spiritually, mentally, physically, bond, and prepare them for what the Creator charged them to be.

You are helping to shape their mind for the journey of their own lives. A huge responsibility that should not be taken lightly. Note that I said a huge responsibility. It's more than just looking at a baby and saying how cute they are, putting on a cute outfit or those nice shoes, taking pictures, and showing them off to family and friends. When you have a child your entire life shifts and if you haven't realized that you have to continuously grow for yourself, you will now. Just when you thought you couldn't love any more than what you already have, this will awaken more. Every ounce of who you are will want the best for this precious gift.

So, get ready.

Get ready for sleepless nights, mommy or daddy being said a million times a day (because they love you so much), busybodies all over the house getting into everything, crying because they are sleepy or want you to pick them up, or crying and you have no idea why. Maybe it's a diaper change, gas, they are cold, they are hungry, they are sick, or they just can't sleep. Also, get ready for those smiles that touch your heart, the hugs just out of the blue, kisses that make your soul just melt, those first steps, the first tooth, the first time they develop their skill of dancing or singing, the constant I love you, and so much more. Looking in your rearview mirror and seeing them fast asleep as you take a ride, when they think they can do your hair like you do theirs, or those first tears you wipe away because they fell down.

At first, you will have no schedule at all and you will just yearn for that moment that you can go to sleep because your little love bug decided that they just wanted to see your sweet face all night. You may just be waiting for the moment that you can just soak in the tub or take a shower because poop or pee may have gotten on you or maybe spit up or milk. Maybe you need to change shirts because the breast milk soaked through the pads while you were asleep. Lots of love. Take a deep breath. It's okay. Smile, brush your hair, and jump right back in there. They will appreciate it. It's a lot but it is so worth it.

QUICK STORY:

I remember when I had my twins. They were so tiny and premature. When we finally got to go home things got very real. I had a c-section which made it very difficult to move around. However, I managed. They had to go back and forth to the testing center because they were having some health issues but aside from that, they were perfect to me. Now, this is where it got real. They were on 2 different schedules. At first, I just went with it. Then I started to get so exhausted. Every 30 minutes one of these little ones was up. One might be hungry, need a diaper change, want to be held, or maybe even burped. Then they would wake up sometimes and cry at the same time. Sometimes I didn't know who I fed and who's diaper I changed because I was so tired. Then one night I said, "That's it." I took a pillow and put them in front of me. I remembered what time I fed 1 of them so I knew that the other would be up shortly and sure enough he was. People may say it's crazy but I did not feed him. I swaddled him, picked him up, and put him inside my shirt close to my heart. He went right back to sleep. Then when it was time for the next feeding, I fed them together, burped them, and changed their diapers. Finally, I was able to sleep for about 2 hours. Best sleep I had since I could remember in a while. This prepared me for the next time. I didn't have twins again but I did have my daughter while the twins were 1 ½. When I got remarried, I had my last 2 children which were 17 to 18 months apart. Thank God I had such a loving and helping husband. He stepped in every time he was home to give baths, make sure that I ate, went to the store, and so much more. None of this was easy.

My husband has pictures of me asleep while I was pumping. He would come and get the baby out of my lap because I would fall asleep in the nursery chair and milk would be everywhere. To be honest it was so hard having 6 children. You have to be very organized and patient. No matter the challenge, I still loved each one of them. That's actually a walk in the park compared to what you will face when they get older. Then you have to hope that all you have taught them kicks in. Show them how valuable they are so they are not searching for that attention from somewhere else. Encouraging them when they feel like they failed you and themselves. Disciplining them when they do the exact opposite of what you taught them. Teaching them how to hold conversations with people, showing them how to save money, how to dress, teaching them about attitude, and so much more. Those conversations you have to have about good touch bad touch because everyone in this world doesn't see them as you do. Educating them about perverts, pedophiles, sex trafficking, and social media. Not just educating but staying attentive so they don't get into any trouble on there. Talking to them about sex, sexually transmitted diseases, or pregnancy is not a very comfortable conversation.

Teaching them how to take care of their body. Praying with them and for them as they go on their journey and experience their own gains and losses in life. Grades in school, first jobs, first dates, sports, learners-permits, driver's license, and girlfriends or boyfriends. It's so much that goes into raising a child. Just because they graduate from high school doesn't mean that your job as a parent is over. Nope. It will continue for the rest of your life. While they are young you have to stay involved. Get to know their friends, where they are, what they are involved in, and take them places so that they will learn how to travel. They will be able to survive on their own because you taught them to but they will still need you. You will be needed for those new experiences that they have never had. When they thought they had the answer and that they knew everything and didn't know anything at all. For they tell you they want to get married and they don't know how to ask or what to do.

The how-to goes into full effect. Yes, they can go online, talk to friends or strangers about how to make things happen but it's something about when they come to you. Hopefully, they will value what you have to say because some don't and just prefer to follow their own will and no matter how many times we tell them that it will make it harder on them; they will not hear you until they hear you (life happens). What if a teen pregnancy occurs or they get an STD that there is no cure for just medication?

Let's get real about these things.

Life will change for both of you.

So now that you have just a portion of what goes on, let's get to the other part.

ASK EACH OTHER:

- Do you want children and if so, how many? Why? If you decide to have several, how will you make time for each of them? (it's not easy)

- Are you going to plan your pregnancies or just let what happens, happen?

- Can you afford to have children? How will this affect your finances or do you care that it will?

- What if you can't have children? Are you willing to adopt? Would you get a surrogate? How about In Vitro Fertilization? What about other methods to get pregnant?

- What if there is a miscarriage? Would you want to try again?

- What are you willing to sacrifice/change in your life for them?

- Are you going to put them in daycare, let them stay with a relative, or keep them with you while you are working?

- Are you sending them to public, private, or home school?

- How will you discipline them?

- What religion are you using for their spiritual base?

- How will you organize your day? How will you make time for each other or just yourself?

- What will you do if your child is born with a disability?

So many questions and I'm not saying have all the answers now but think about it. It's impossible to know everything but very important to get all the information that you can. I mean really, think about things that most don't want to talk about. What do you do if your spouse passes away and it's just you and the baby? Do not leave your babies with just anyone. I don't care how desperate you may feel. One night could turn into your worst nightmare. I know that it gets tough and you just really may need a break but you don't want them to have to fight someone much larger than them. You never know what type of patience a person has, if they like touching small children, are abusive, or anything else that could be going on with them.

Pay attention and choose well.

What about a blended family? What if you met someone or are with someone that has children from a prior relationship? Most people say; "I will love them like my own." That is true but what if they don't want you to. What if they just can't stand you and everything that came with you? All they can see is they want their parents to get back together and are wondering why you are here. On the other hand: What if they just love you so much that they wrap their arms around you and call you Mom or Dad? How would you feel? How will you bond with them?

Here are some things to think about:

- How will you handle rejection?

- How will you handle discipline?

- What if you and your spouse disagree on certain things about the children?

- How will you handle the non-custodial parent? How will you handle the situation if there is no child support?

- How will you handle the non-custodial parent when it comes down to making your own plans and they decide that they don't care about your plans but want to show up when they are ready?

- How will you handle the heart of those children if or when that non-custodial parent lets them down by telling them they are coming and not showing up

- How will you help them to heal while you, the non-biological parent, are healing from those hurtful words or actions just because you are there?

- How will your schedule change?

- What are you willing to do to have them in your life?

- What if it all goes well and it is like one big happy family? Awesome! That is not always the case but in some cases, they do try to make it all work for the children.

I'm not just talking about a blended family just because I heard about it. I have lived it and we continue to walk this journey out. My husband has done such a great job. He stepped right in and when I say he has been all in. I mean it. No matter what happened, he was a trooper. He stepped in when I had 4 children and worked with tears, anger, fears, and some tough words. When they were sick or needed something he was there. I thank my Creator every day for him. People don't like to talk about the issues that may step on some toes. These are real conversations that people don't tend to have because the first thought is that it's going to work. That is the best attitude and heart to have for it. It will come together but you guys are going to have to work really hard. If need be, seek help from others who have been there before or maybe counseling if it's really hard. Be patient with them and realize this is their first go around too. Time heals wombs and a whole lot of love. Talk and love them through it.

It's not easy with children because they don't know how to convey their feeling so some may act out. Be patient with them and try your best to find out where they are with their feelings. Handle them how you would want someone to handle you. They are little people. They didn't come here for you to yell in their face, curse them out, slap around, take out your frustration on, for you to share every secret that they share with you with others, to put them down because of their mistakes, or shut them down when they really need you to build them up. Talk to them. Ask them questions. See what they think about the world and why. Even when they are little. It's very interesting.

QUICK STORY:

I remember walking with 2 of my children who at the time were 3 and 4. I was giving them a chance to walk around because they had been inside all day. While we were walking, they started to talk about

Halloween. They had watched it on kids youtube. So, I took the opportunity to have a conversation to see what they thought about it. As I had gotten older, I decided that I would no longer celebrate this day with my children because it didn't make any sense. I had done some reading on it and I just felt like this was not something I wanted my children doing although we had done it many times before. Anyway, our 4-year-old said that she could not wait to get a costume. I asked her; "For what?" She told me that she wanted to dress up as Doc McStuffins and get candy. Our son let me know that he wanted to be a construction worker. I asked them; "Why?" She kept skipping and then she said; "I don't know." Our son said; "Because I want to use the digger." I know our daughter loves Doc McStuffins and wants to be a doctor and our son always gets excited when we pass by a construction site. Mind you, we had already bought the jacket and doctor bag that went to Doc McStuffins as well as the electric riding tractor for our son. I know she admired this wonderful character and that our son loved construction which I thought was pretty cool. However, I still wanted to see what they thought about it in reference to Halloween. So, I asked; "Why do they give you candy for Halloween?" They both said that they didn't know. I said well I know we taught you not to take candy from strangers so why would you want to go up to a stranger's house and get candy. Our daughter stopped walking and turned and looked at me. She said; "I don't know." I said; Think about it, people put on costumes of who they want to be for the day and knock on doors to get candy. Do people want to be bears, witches, pumpkins, and monsters?" She said, "No." Our son of course said yes.

Then our daughter said; "I think people just want the candy mommy." The moral of the story is to talk and ask questions. Your kids may be too young to talk about some things but meet them where they are. See what they think. It may surprise you.

You really want to ask them what they think about something they are actively participating in or that they bring up to you so you can make sure they have a healthy understanding of things. Kids do not have a filter. They will tell you if they like something or not. Don't forget to have fun!!! They are only little for so long. Trust me, it passes by so fast.

Let me touch on some other subjects when it comes down to new little ones and blended families. Something people don't want to talk about is changes of the body, the time for each other, and jealousy. Ladies and Gents remember that having a baby does change the body. Some women are able to bounce back quicker than others and some never go back the same. You may see stretch marks or loose skin. For those that breastfeed, their breast may be full during that time but after they may go down a few sizes and the skin may change. Some women continue to have a pooch (the bottom part of the stomach under the navel that kind of sticks out. Yes, this does happen. Now men if you see a little hair on the floor or in the shower, that is normal. A lot of times our hair grows and gets full and thick during the pregnancy but afterward, it just sheds and sheds. That is just Postpartum hair loss (telogen effluvium). It will bounce back so no need to worry. Hormones had to change so guess what, they have to go back.

Cesarean sections are tough. Trust me I know; I have 6 children but I've had 5 c-sections. I hope you have that pillow handy because if you decide to laugh hard, cough, or even if your body needs to let out a sudden sneeze; you will need it. Trying to pee for the first time will seem strange and getting around will take you just a little longer. Don't be afraid to ask for some help. If you decide not to breastfeed, let's just say hop in the shower for some relief because that milk will need to go somewhere. Your breast will become engorged and it will hurt. Maybe get a hot rag, squeeze the milk out, pump, or put some cabbage on it (something I heard but not sure if it works). I found that nursing was better and that you solidify your bond with your baby. If you decide to breastfeed, leave some time for dad. Share with dad the opportunity to burp your little love bug. He wants to be a part of it too.

QUICK STORY:

Jealousy

I remember when my siblings and I were little and we would ask my Mom for help with our homework. She would come down to help and try to explain some of the problems as best she could. Within that moment my Dad would get so mad at her and start yelling at her for helping. He would say every time I turn around you are down there with those children. So, we ended up doing a lot of things on our own. We grew up trying to figure it out. That was not easy. Mind you other kids, as well as adults, can be cruel. They don't care that you have to go through whatever it is and learn alone. They pick at your lessons and call you everything they can think of but never thinking that you may need some help.

My Dad always felt like my Mom should be where he was. We found out from the streets what we should have found out at home. That was what it was. So, Parent's make sure you are prepared. Make sure you schedule time. If you see your spouse is helping the kids maybe lend a hand and it will go by faster. Be helpers one to another. They did not have your precious babies by themselves. Also, you have been here much longer than they have so I'm pretty sure they are trying to figure this world out. Don't leave them to a world that you decided to bring them into. Work as a team to get things done so that they have a healthy balance and a chance to see that both of their parents are there for them. This builds their trust. Parents should want their children to do well. The goal is to raise your children in such a way that they are like eagles.

Over time they can fly on their own.

Job, Self-Employed, or Both

Colossians 3:23 (NLT)

23 Work willingly at whatever you do, as though you were working for the Lord rather than for people.

Deuteronomy 24:14-15 (AMP)

14 "You shall not take advantage of a hired servant who is poor and needy, whether [he is] one of your countrymen or one of the strangers (resident aliens, foreigners) who is in your land inside your cities. 15 You shall give him his wages on the day that he earns them before the sun sets—for he is poor and is counting on it—so that he does not cry out to the Lord against you, and it becomes a sin for you.

Psalm 90:17 (AMP)

17 And let the [gracious] favor of the Lord our God be on us; Confirm for us the work of our hands— Yes, confirm the work of our hands.

Psalm 128:2 (AMP)

2 For you shall eat the fruit of [the labor of] your hands, You will be happy and blessed and it will be well with you

This can be a tricky conversation especially when you are already established with your career. Depending on the situation (moving, staying at home, starting a new business) you decide to stay or leave.

ASK THESE QUESTIONS:

- Do I make enough money to support my family in the event of my spouse losing their job?
- Does my job have benefits? Which job has the lowest cost of benefits?
- Is my job closer to where we live or will it cost us more to commute?
- Do I leave or do you? Why?

- Are we working on a business together? What kind?

- If I leave my job how will we make ends meet and are you okay with taking care of us? Will we be able to save, travel, or take care of a family with whatever decision we make?

- If I am terminated or the business that I have started goes under, what will we do? You do what's best for your family. Make sure to have these conversations even if it feels uncomfortable.

The honest thing I can say about this is if you make a decision don't let people outside of your home make you feel bad.

QUICK STORY:

I remember when I left my job and made a decision to start over people had so much to say. The key thing is they had so much to say but nothing to contribute. It's okay if they are just checking on you, don't get me wrong. Honestly, if they are not paying your bills then they should not be counting your cost. See that is where I had sunk. I allowed people to make me feel bad because I had chosen to be a domestic engineer (stay-at-home mom). I felt as though I was such a burden until I built my own confidence back up. It is your choice. You count the cost. You make the decision. You guys together.

Family Members & Friends

Proverbs 12:26 (NLT)

26 The godly give good advice to their friends; the wicked lead them astray.

Proverbs 16:28 (NLT)

28 A troublemaker plants seeds of strife; gossip separates the best of friends.

Proverbs 18:24 (NLT)

24 There are "friends" who destroy each other, but a real friend sticks closer than a brother.

This is one of my favorites. You may say why would this be a favorite to anyone. Well, this is who your spouse was around most times before you even came in the picture. Sometimes people don't even make it to marriage because of this or it makes their relationship very hard to maintain. Everyone will not be singing your praises because you have this newfound love. Some friends and family will never like the person that you are with. It may not even be because of anything that they have done but just because. Who knows...Have you ever seen those movies where the mother-in-law or father-in-law didn't like the spouse? Or the friend that didn't want their friend to get married because they wanted to keep them to themselves.

Let's dig in.

Now that I have your attention I will go ahead and just tell you this.

My husband is my best friend before anyone or anything. I will go to bat for him like no other. I have his front back and both sides. Say something to him and you might as well have said it to me. He is my ace boon coon, my homie lover friend, travel partner, and everything else you could think of. He is God's gift to me as I am to him. I don't take him for granted and I love him very much. I am the protector of his heart along with God. I share in wanting to spend the rest of our lives together.

On the flip side of that, God gives us family. He also gives us friends that become family. My husband is not a replacement for my family and friends but he is a great addition. If you are very close to your family and friends this is a great topic. How will you handle your family asking you for money when your accounts are combined? What about an unexpected visit?

Our family and friends are the first ones that introduce us to love and loyalty. We learn how to rely on, trust, build, hustle, dress, cook, clean, and so much more. They are also resources. Most of you can trust them with your life and everything in it. Although this is all true, things do change when you get into a relationship.

Your time spent with others will not be the same. I don't care what you say. Trust me. What happens when they want to go out or go to a different church than what you would normally go to? Mind you that you used to pick your friend up every Sunday. See, change. Not a bad thing but something to be discussed. What if you were used to sharing everything with your friend and now you just want to keep a little to yourself when they asked you what you did last night? Do you tell them everything?

No!!! I just want to say this before we even get started.

Now, if someone is abusive to you verbally or physically then that is not what I'm talking about. I am talking about those little arguments that occur and though it might be tense you know that you will be right back together. Why? Well, when you forgive your spouse your family or friends will not be on the same page with you. When they see you are back together, they will say I thought you were upset with them. What are you guys doing back together? There will be some residual because they get protective of you. Your sex life should not be at the top of your discussion board either. What you and your spouse do is between the 2 of you not for the world. Be careful with the information you give out.

Our parents, siblings, and friends are our support group. They are there to help us along the way. Remember I said a resource early on and that's exactly what I meant. Ask them questions about how to do things that you don't know how to do. Maybe you don't know how to cook something and your parents do or maybe someone used to be a stripper and you want to learn how to do that for your spouse; Ask. The alternative is youtube, google, bing, books, or take classes. If you run into a problem as far as how to communicate with your spouse about something or you guys have a certain issue that comes up. Ask questions. You don't have to give out all your information to get information unless that is something that you have decided to do.

There are ways to ask a question.

For example:

- If you have a problem with this or that (whatever the problem is), how do you fix it

- How do you bake a cake that will rise?

- How did you nurse your baby, did it hurt, were you scared when you had your first kid? (those close to you will know that this means you may need help or you are just curious)

- How did you know your spouse was the one?

- What was your first time like? Was it painful? Did you everything to do?

- Would you date someone that had been abused as a child? Why?

- I was listening to this or that or reading and just wondered what your thoughts on it would be. Tell me about your marriage: How and when you met dad, mom, grandpa, or grandma?

- How did you make your marriage last so long? Or why did your marriage end? Was any of it hard? What did you do when it was?

- How did you raise us the way that you did?

Here is the thing. You know your family and they know you. Your spouse is learning who they are and they may not want to feel like everyone knows how they just made love to you and everything they did to you or maybe they didn't finish because it wouldn't stay erect. Those are things that only you and your spouse should be blushing about or talking about. They may not want the world to know that they lost their job or everything that happened to them when they were young. Some things are just for you guys to share. Now some people are wide open and they don't mind. For me, I would just let them tell it on their own if they would like to but I will not be the one sharing someone's personal life experience.

You will have to set boundaries for those that don't know how to do it themselves. If someone needs to call you late at night it should be an emergency. Some things go on in a person's home at night or maybe during the day (sex, sleep, sick babies, guest) that deserve your respect as well as your friends and families.

When you get in a relationship this doesn't mean that now it's time to get rid of my friends and find me some new ones. Most times our friends are very understanding and they want to see us happy. They can't wait to see God produce in your life. This will show you those true and loyal friends. At every moment they are standing there ready to applaud you and help where they can. They celebrate you and they are honest with you even if they don't agree with what you are doing or saying. They know just how to say it to you that will help you to see where they are coming from. Those are friendships you don't want to lose. I have heard people say; "I'm not giving up my friends for anyone or giving up my family for anyone." My question for them is; "Who asked you to do that? Why would they ask you to do that?" Unless someone is trying to control you or something is going on that will hurt you then I don't know why someone would do that. You guys have an understanding, right?

LET'S ASK SOME QUESTIONS HERE:

- Are you okay with your spouse having friends of the opposite sex?

- Are you okay with your spouse hanging out until after midnight or coming home the next day?

- Are you comfortable with your spouse spending the night at their friend's house even if it is the opposite sex?
- Do you trust your spouse to do the right thing if they are hanging with their friends and the turn-up gets real?
- Can you trust it if they are drinking?

- Are you okay with your spouse's friend spending the night at your home that you share?

- What boundaries have you set up so that there is a balance to your friendship?

- If something happens and their friend needs financial help or a place to stay, are you comfortable with them coming to stay with you guys?

- Are you okay with them coming to dinner with you guys even if they don't have a date to bring of their own?

- Would you be okay leaving your friend at the house with your spouse?

- Are you okay with your spouse hanging out with single people all the time? (A lot of times the conversation is different.)

You may say yes to all of these questions and say they should trust me or I'm not here to deal with an insecure person. Maybe you are not the person or maybe you do need to figure out what trust is. Some of these things have nothing to do with trust or being insecure. Being married or in a relationship is about a lot of things but respect and boundaries are major. Just know that the same thing you can do, so can the other. If this is not resolved it can definitely lead to some major problems in your relationship. While you are getting to know each other, this is the part that I mentioned in: **Who is He/She** portion that is very important. Also, in the **Know thyself** portion.

Now if you are married and didn't know to ask these questions this is going to be hard but you guys can make it. Maybe you have new friends that you have met on the job, at your kid's school, at the store, or through networking. Discuss these things with each other and don't let this be the part where you guys can't compromise. Better yet, try to link up with people that are in relationships or married. They may have a healthier understanding of your time and limitations.

Before you get married if you have any friends' you guys function in a certain type of way. Depending on who you are and what you like to do, there has been some type of bond created. You guys may just go on vacation together, hang out at each other's house, have casual drinks at a restaurant or get completely drunk until you pass out, club all night, sit on the phone and talk for hours, text all day, go to family events together, go to church together, go shopping or study together, work out together, laugh at the most craziest things, share eventful things such as someone new you are dating, your wedding day, or having your first kid. You see it's like family.

These are most likely lifelong friends.

Sometimes they are more like family than your biological family. Once again depending on where you come from. They are around us because they want to be not because they have to be. True friends know your darkest secrets, have seen you at your worst, have wiped tears from your face, laughed until you couldn't anymore, have argued with you and called you a few minutes later or the next day, have supported you when you fell to your lowest point, and so much more. They never share your information with anyone. What is that saying? Your friend will take it to the grave with them. They value and appreciate you. I mean you guys could have not spoken for weeks and you know that you are still friends and that you each have a life that may be full. However, you will send them a text just to check in and make sure everything is okay. Some spouses may look at this relationship and develop their own opinion of all this and feel as though they should take the place of your friend. They may feel jealous or not secure. Yes, just in case you were wondering: This does happen. Even to the point that they don't want you to hang out with that particular friend anymore. Sometimes it's jealousy or insecurities, maybe they just don't agree with you hanging out all times of the night because they don't want anything to happen to you, and sometimes they actually see something that you don't see because it's the normal thing you have done for years.

Let's talk about that friend, sibling, or parent that was there for all those years until you met someone and started sharing with them how happy you are. Happens all the time. They get very upset because they are still single and here it is another wedding they are going to and it's not them getting married. Maybe you getting into a relationship takes away you giving your time and money to them. There could be numerous things. Be careful because if they are feeling this way, they will not be the best support for you during this time. Also, you could have that friend, sibling, or parent that is married just like you but their marriage is on the rocks. All the while yours is going great and you start to tell them about how great it is and they are just not feeling it. The moment that you go through something with your spouse they are waiting to tell you to do the very thing that they won't do themselves. Say this or say that, if I were you; I would have done this or that, or you should leave. Listen out for this because they are still there with their husband. They will have you saying all this and sowing seeds of discord and before you know it you are single and they are still married. Then it's I'm so sorry that happened to you, I hope you meet someone new, or sorry I can't talk to you because my husband/wife and I are about to go out on a date. Those words saying don't feel lonely, God will take care of it. How about do you have any money I can borrow or can I use your car to go see my boyfriend?

You have to have these conversations not just with your spouse but with your friends and family too. They all want to be a part of your life. How do you make it all fit? Get organized and see how much time you will have and how much happier you will be.

Goal Setting

Habakkuk 2:2-3 (AMP)

(2) And the Lord answered me and said, Write the vision and make it plain (engrave it so plainly up tablets that everyone who passes may be able to read it (3) For the vision is yet for an appointed time and it hastens to the end [fulfillment]; it will not deceive or disappoint. Though it tarry, wait [earnestly] for it, because it will surely come; it will not be behindhand on its appointed day.

Have personal goals as well as goals together. Set a time frame of when you want these things to be done. Don't just let them linger around and never get the opportunity to feel the accomplishment. Goals are for all things. Not just finances. That's weight loss, children, travel, friends, and just all-around your life.

I have heard people say to make a 5-10-15-20-year plan. I also remember my teachers telling up to write out where we saw ourselves in the next 5 years. Well, I think that these plans are great to start out with. Make sure you are specific with what your goal is. Set goals for career advancement, finishing school, starting your own business, what level of learning you would like your kids to be on by a certain time, weight loss, travel, finances, investments, and more. It's up to you. It is so important to make them realistic and to keep them in front of you.

Make it a priority to go back and write out what prevented you from reaching a certain goal and make new ones. Never just take a goal off of your sheet. Leave it there to come back to or to see if that goal may evolve into something that is connected to a future goal. Don't let excuses cause you not to reach a goal. Always research so that you know what is required to reach a goal so you are not left there disappointed in the outcome.

What could change your goals:

- Loss of a job
- Increase in finances

- A new baby
- Loss of a spouse
- Not doing the proper research
- Not staying focused, stagnant, complacent
- No longer Interested
- Not willing to work together to accomplish them
- Someone gets sick

Think about all these things. Set goals that even with these potential obstacles there you can still do them. Also, remember that just because it doesn't happen in the time and space that you want it that the goal is no good. We show God our way and He has a way of showing us His way. That doesn't make this goal unobtainable. It just takes a little patience, work, and time. Don't be so hard on yourself. Just keep pushing and at its appointed time it will happen.

Zechariah 4:10 (KJV)

Do not despise the day of small beginnings, for the Lord rejoices to see the work begin

Even trees start off as a seed and some take about 20 years to reach maturity. Bamboo is planted and watered and it takes about 5 years before you see anything. Everything takes time. Give yourself time!!!

Marriage

Genesis 2:24-25 (AMP)

(24) Therefore, a man shall leave his father and his mother and shall become united and cleave to his wife, and they shall become one flesh. (25) And the man and his wife were both naked and were not embarrassed or ashamed in each other's presence

I still remember these words spoken:

The traditional vows...

I, _____, take you, _____, to be my lawfully wedded (husband/wife), to have and to hold, from this day forward, for better, for worse, for richer, for poorer, in sickness and in health, until death do us part.

What a mouth full of soulful meaningful words. Every word is intertwined with what you will share for the rest of your lives. A true journey ordained by your very own Creator.

Genesis 2:24-25 (AMP)

(24) Therefore, a man shall leave his father and his mother and shall become united and cleave to his wife, and they shall become one flesh. (25) And the man and his wife were both naked and were not embarrassed or ashamed in each other's presence

Here it's just a simple as it is written. Not just by the fact of you leaving your father and mother but being naked. The naked part doesn't just mean your physical body but with what you feel, what's on your mind, where you came from, how you process things, and so much more.

Most of you may be wondering why this is last. Well, it takes all of what you read and then some to get to this point and during this union. This is not for the weak at heart. You will work your hardest. It will take everything that you have to get to the point of coasting together.

My husband and I have both been married before, we both got married young, we have a blended family [he has a son, I have 4 children, and we share 2 children together (we love them equally)], we had to learn on our own about finances (still learning), and we have had to go through a lot just to get to where we are. It has not been easy.

We stand true to these words:

Matthew 19:6 (AMP)

So they are no longer two, but one flesh. What therefore God has joined together, let not man put asunder (separate)

It means so much to me for him to trust me and know that I care about everything pertaining to him. He matters to me. I matter to me. My children matter to me. My family matters to me. I had written an article on my blog that I would like to share with you:

Selflove & Keeping it Fresh During Your Marriage: Conversations with My King Written

August 23, 2018

My husband and I were talking about how easy it is to stop taking out time for yourself when you get married and start a family. It seems even harder when you come in and have children prior to the marriage because you somewhat miss out on the honeymoon part. Newly-weds get to come home and break in the new house and those that are in a relationship know exactly what I mean (sex everywhere and anytime). Let's be real, you get to have the pure freedom of having the entire house to yourselves and do whatever, whenever, and however you want without wondering who can see or hear you. This may not apply to all but more often than people talk about.

Now in this day, you don't always have grandparents or siblings to watch your children so you can date or do other things that come along with having a marriage. Back in the day, you had Big Mama or those siblings that really had the time to be there. Things were structured more around the family unit. Now, most grandparents are still working and most siblings are not just working but working doubles and secondary jobs to make ends meet. Life is not so much focused on the family unit but survival for most. So, how do you put aside time for yourself as well as time for your spouse so that you are not just maintaining but keeping your relationship as well as your own love for yourself fresh?

Well, here we go... you know how you get out of a relationship you seem to find your best you. It seems as if you get in shape, eat better, find the time to go out more, become adventurous, travel more, treat yourself, get your hair done or haircut more often, get creative, speak more candidly, and so many other things. Why? Why not be all of that in the relationship that you are in? What stopped you from being that person during your relationship? Why not be that to you and your spouse? Those parts of you are so important and vital to your relationship. Those parts of you are not just important for your spouse but for you and your children.

We talked about how our kids need to not only hear us talk about doing things but for the moments that we can show them. they need to see us not just at home but out and about so that they know how to conduct themselves, how to speak to people, how to handle certain situations. They need to know how to communicate and move around. They need to learn not just from school how to be creative, how to search for things, how to research their history, how to read, how to make friends, how to dance, how to communicate, and how to be themselves but from us. They need to see you guys be and do all those things together and when you are out alone. They need to see you laugh until you can't laugh anymore, dance when a beat moves your soul, eat healthily, get upset, work out, make friends, and be there for others and not just yourselves. Not just your children but you need to do all those things for yourself. You need to do all that for your spouse.

Let's be honest if all you do is go to work and come home what type of conversations are you having. You have to get out and even if it's to take a walk at the park or the neighborhood. You are able to talk about the birds, the kids at the park, the weather, people you had a chance to meet, and how you felt while you were out. You can keep it fresh even with limitations. Walk around the store, try on something that you may want to see yourself in or that you want your spouse to see you in. Some of it is free and some will only cost you a little gas and you will spend that on something that is just an impulse buy such as fast food. Look on youtube and find a new hairstyle, something to learn and share with your spouse, or even a new dance. Make time even if it's just 30 minutes.

People with very large families tend to put things off a lot which is understandable and so do small families when it's necessary to do so. We know because we have a very large family. We often focus on what the kids need, the bills, business needs, the house, the school, and so much more. Don't get me wrong, all those things are so important and very much so a priority but so are we. Not just as individuals but as a unit. All of what you have existed because by God you were able to come together and build. You were able to fall in love. How?!!? Making Time!!! It was a number, a phone call, a date, a pursuit, spontaneous sex, and many other things. You were building something. The beginning was the foundation and the rest was the other parts of the house. What about making it into a home? The both of you make the house a home. Your bond together as well as your individuality. Why did you fall in love with that person? You liked certain things about them.

So, both the individual parts as well as the parts we share together play a role in our Kingdom. Even if you have a large family or you work a lot you can set aside time for the two of you. How? When the kids are in bed surprise your spouse by putting on a little music, pouring a glass of wine or whatever they prefer, and slow dance with them or for them. When you can get a family member or friend that you trust to come over and watch the kids for an hour or so and go to the movies. If you don't have that, cook something special for that person. Run a bubble bath with candles and soft music and get in it together. Give each other a massage. Have a day where you just hang out on the couch watching movies and that way even if the kids are running around you guys are right there but you're spending time together. Flirt throughout the day by sending some text that may make them blush or smile throughout the day. Make a call just to say I love you or I'm thinking of you. Sit on the porch and talk about goals, dreams, what inspires each other, what you want, and what you need. Sit and just listen to the other person talk. Take out the time to continue building. Some of those things you can also do for yourself.

Marriage requires a friendship.

The ability to be angry and still love through it even when you don't want to put any more energy into it. It will need your focus. Growth is mandatory. Grow past what was and develop into what is. Be willing to be there and practice daily forgiveness as you learn who you are together. Trust is so important in order to move your relationship forward. Prayer is there for covering, direction, connection, enhancement, binding, refreshing you daily, and for those times that you can't see (See, Endure, Empower) each other. Be patient and support each other. Not one is greater than the other because without each other you can't have a relationship.

Now that you have made it here let's see if you can answer these questions:

- Are you willing to try?
- Are you willing to let me come through the wall?
- Do we need some help trying to figure this out?
- Are we able to forgive and move forward (does not just happen overnight)?
- How can we do this? What do you need from me?
- What do I need for myself in order to move forward?

Ecclesiastes 4:9-12 (AMP)

9Two are better than one because they have a more satisfying return for their labor; 10for if either of them falls, the one will lift up his companion. But woe to him who is alone when he falls and does not have another to lift him up. 11 Again, if two lie down together, then they keep warm; but how can one be warm alone? 12 And though one can overpower him who is alone, two can resist him. A cord of three strands is not quickly broken.

Ready!!! Set!!! Goal!!!

Goal Your Way to a Successful Happy Marriage

Habakkuk 2:2

Write the Vision, Make It Plain

The Goal: Him & Her=Happily Married

Get your calendars ready, pens, tablets, phones, pencils, paper, vision boards, and whatever else you need to get started.

It's time to take a look at some things.

Set some goals each day, week, month, and year. Be serious about what you want.

When you want to go to a store that everyone is talking about and you have never been there before, "What do you do?" You use your GPS, map, or ask for directions. Don't be afraid to get some directions to a place that you have never been or tried to get to and didn't make it there successfully. Being an entrepreneur you will work harder for yourself than anyone else because this is your baby. Well, this is your life. Work hard at it. If your child needed something you would work hard at it. Your marriage or relationship is your baby. You may or may not have planned it but here it is.

What are you going to do?

www.ingramcontent.com/pod-product-compliance
Lightning Source LLC
Chambersburg PA
CBHW071315060426
42444CB00036B/2873